The Holy One of Israel

Exploring Isaiah

S. D. Ellison

DEDICATION

For Antrim Baptist Church

It is a privilege to preach and teach the Scriptures;
It is a joy to do so for such an encouraging and gracious
church family.

CONTENTS

ACKNOWLEDGMENTS

I must begin by acknowledging my wife, Tracy. There is no doubt that without her help and support I would never have been afforded the same opportunity to study, preach, and teach. She is tireless in her encouragement and constant in her love. I praise God for such a partner in life, love, and ministry.

I am also grateful to both Tom Moore and Tracy for reading earlier drafts of this book. Both of them have a keen eye for accuracy, detail, and good writing. This book is certainly better for their input.

Finally, I wish to mention Antrim Baptist Church. They were brave enough to grant me an opportunity to minister among them, kind enough to welcome Tracy and I with open arms, and exemplify longsuffering by remaining with me as I preached 66 chapters in only five sermons. It is because of their goodness and patience towards me that I gladly dedicate this book to them.

Of course, all of the above are simply good gifts from the Holy One of Israel, and so all praise and glory is His alone.

INTRODUCTION:
TREADING THE SAME OLD PATHS

One of my fondest memories from my school days is completing my Duke of Edinburgh expeditions. There were six of us who were good friends, and perhaps more surprisingly, remained so throughout all three expeditions. It was delightful to enjoy the great outdoors with good friends. We began in the Glens of Antrim, progressed to the Mourne Mountains, and finally graduated to the outstandingly beautiful Lake District. Since then I have always maintained a passing interest in hill-walking, even voluntarily camping out on a few occasions. Living in Northern Ireland, the Mournes are obviously the destination of choice.

Despite being competent with a compass and a map, and the almost endless options of routes through the Mournes, I often find myself returning the same track. Each and every time I make my way to the Mournes, I park in the same car park, walk the same forest path, and scale the summit of the same mountain, Slieve Donard. To the neglect of all the other routes, I find myself treading the same old path.

In an attempt to justify this monotony, I assure myself that since I have made the effort to be here it is sensible to scale the summit of the highest mountain (2, 790 ft./850 m. above sea level). The reality, however, is that there is something comforting about being familiar with your surroundings. There is a little nostalgia about returning to somewhere you know. It is easy to tread the same old path.

There is nothing necessarily wrong with all of that. But it is a little limiting. In my mind the Mourne Mountains have only one vista, that from the top of Slieve Donard. Yet, this is not an accurate picture, because the Mourne Mountains have hundreds, if not thousands of vistas. I just haven't taken the time or the effort to explore them.

All too often this is how we treat the book of Isaiah. There is so much to see in Isaiah. There are endless avenues to be explored, various aspects to be meditated upon, and some of the most spectacular vistas in all of Scripture to observe. Yet, again and again, we return to tread the same old paths. Please don't mistake me, the vistas of Isaiah 6, 9, and 53 are spectacular. As is the vista from the top of Slieve Donard. But there is so much more to see.

Exploring all of Isaiah in-depth would take too long, and is not the aim here. Rather, I hope to point the reader in the direction of a number of other lesser known vistas in Isaiah and to offer a broad framework to aid our personal reading of this massive book. First, despite the grandeur of Isaiah 6, the wonder of Isaiah 9, and, the emotion of Isaiah 53, we often do Isaiah a disservice by simply treading these same old paths. There are numerous vistas that are equally as stunning as these familiar chapters, and I hope to point them out on the way through. Second, even though I have been to Bible college, and preach and teach regularly, I have often found it difficult to place individual chapters into the grand flow of the book of Isaiah. Year after year, as I reach Isaiah in my daily reading plan, I struggle to see the book in its entirety. Part of the problem is that its size hampers our ability to see the big picture clearly. I pray that this book may offer some guidance on that front.

With all this in mind, I am going to present the grand sweep of Isaiah in five movements that will give us both the flow and the big picture of the book. Come and tread some less familiar ground with me.

THE HOLY ONE OF ISRAEL & HIS PEOPLE
(ISAIAH 1-12)

The Holy One of Israel

Names are important. They are important for a variety of reasons. Names distinguish people from one another. Names have meaning. Remembering individuals' names helps them feel important, known, loved. Names are important to us, they are important to God, and that means they are important to Isaiah.

There is one name for God that is a particular favourite of Isaiah, Holy One of Israel. This name for God appears 31 times in the Old Testament, and 25 of those appearances are in Isaiah.[1] Isaiah's desire, it seems, is to make the reader aware that the God of Israel is distinct. He is holy. This is pressed home with other titles, such as "Holy God" (5:16) and "Holy One" (10:17). Added to this is the

---

[1] Isa. 1:4; 5:19, 24; 10:20; 12:6; 17:7; 29:19; 30:11, 12, 15; 31:1; 37:23; 41:14, 16, 20; 43:3, 14; 45:11; 47:4; 48:17; 49:7; 54:5; 55:5; 60:9, 14.

famous vision of Isaiah 6, in which God is pronounced as holy, holy, holy (6:3). This name, Holy One of Israel, is important because it impresses upon the reader the reality of who the God of Israel really is. He is utterly unique, perfectly pure, completely other, the most regal and beautiful of all. He is the Holy One of Israel.

The importance of this name is that God's very own people must be like him. They must be distinct, unique, and pure to bear the name of God's people. Notice, after all, God is not simply the Holy One, but the Holy One of Israel. Thus, Israel must be holy like their God. In the opening twelve chapters Isaiah elaborates on this relationship between the Holy One of Israel and his people.

Rebellion

It is somewhat shocking to observe Isaiah initially using the term rebellion to summarise the relationship between the Holy One of Israel and his people. The opening chapter makes for dire reading, as Isaiah makes it clear that God's very own people are in rebellion against him. Even though the Holy One of Israel had brought up the nation of Israel, they rebelled (v. 2), forsaking and despising him. The nation is engaged in vain worship, full of iniquity, evil and injustice (vv. 12-17). Israel has prostituted herself, housing murderers, thieves, and accepting bribes (vv. 21-23). Five times in this opening chapter Isaiah calls the Holy One of Israel's very own people rebels (vv. 2, 5, 20, 23, 28). The impetus of this chapter is that God's very own people are turning away from him. In Isaiah 1 the sin of God's people is brutally exposed – they are in rebellion.

This rebellion is evidenced in more detail in chapter five as Isaiah sings a song. In the song of a vineyard (5:1-7)

Isaiah depicts God as a gardener caring lovingly for his vineyard. After caring so tenderly for his vineyard, the gardener rightly expects a harvest of good grapes. But instead he gets wild grapes (vv. 2, 4). By good grapes Isaiah means justice and righteous, but the harvest was bloodshed and outcries (v. 7). The Holy One of Israel expected a holy harvest. Instead, his very own people served up a harvest of rebellion. They bound themselves to wickedness, indulged in perversion of justice, and revelled in pride and drunkenness (vv. 18-23).

The book of Isaiah begins by unmistakeably asserting that the Holy One of Israel's very own people, the nation of Israel, are in rebellion. The reason this is so scandalous is because this rebellion is against the One who has brought them up, tended to them lovingly, and rightly expected obedience. The rebellion is shocking because it is against the Holy One of Israel. The seriousness of the rebellion correlates with the status of the one being rebelled against.

When is the last time you heard it reported on the news that an elderly lady had her handbag stolen? I am sure it has been a while, if ever. Hundreds, if not thousands of elderly ladies across the United Kingdom must have their handbags stolen every day. Yet it never makes it to the news. But suppose the Queen had her handbag stolen – that would be front-page news, the top story on any news bulletin, and undoubtedly trend on social media. Why? Because it is the Queen! The status of the individual determines the magnitude of the action. No one knows Maud down the street, and so when her handbag is stolen no one cares. Everyone knows who Her Majesty is, and so if her handbag ever got stolen everyone would care.

Likewise with the Holy One of Israel. His people's rebellion is significant because of his status. As David Jackman points out: "For Isaiah, the exaltation of God's holiness and the recognition of our deep sin are inextricably bound together as inseparable strands of the same spiritual reality."[2] This link is established at the outset by Isaiah – sin (especially that of God's own people) is serious because it is against the Holy One of Israel.

The reader of Isaiah, then, must wrestle with the realisation that our sin is rebellion against the Holy One of Israel. The sin of God's people is a rejection of God and his ways. It is of the utmost significance. Not because of who we are, nor even necessarily because of what we have done, but because of who God is – holy, holy, holy. Our sin, our rebellion, is an assault on God's character (for we are his people) and that makes it serious.

The implication is that every sin is serious. Jesus makes this very same point himself during his Sermon on the Mount. Just because you haven't murdered anyone doesn't make you better than the murderer, because you still get angry (Matt. 5:21-22). Just because you haven't been sexually active with someone who isn't your spouse doesn't make you better than the adulterer, because you still lust (5:27-30). It isn't the sin, it is the person sinned against that makes it serious. More, the Holy One of Israel is the only one who is always sinned against in every sin.

Isaiah is at pains to make this clear from the very beginning of his book. Everything that unfolds in the book

---

[2] David Jackman, *Teaching Isaiah: Unlocking Isaiah for the Bible Teacher* (Ross-shire: Christian Focus Publications, 2010), 65.

from this point on is either as a consequence or in response to this issue.

Judgement

The immediate consequence in the opening twelve chapters to this rebellion is judgement. The reality of judgement is scattered throughout these chapters, with almost every chapter making some mention of it.

We see it, for example, in Isaiah 2:12-19 as Isaiah speaks about "a day". Isaiah's initial listeners and readers did not understand each day as a repetition, or a revolution of the globe. Rather, they understood each new day to be another step forward towards a particular day: The Day of the LORD. This particular day was to be a day of judgement. A day when wrongs would be righted, wickedness would be eradicated, and righteousness would be celebrated. That is the day spoken about in Isaiah 2:12-19. There the Holy One of Israel asserts his intentions to humble the proud, even if they are his very own people, because he alone should be exalted (v. 17).

This judgement is expanded upon, at length, in 3:1-4:1. It is a terrifying passage as we read of the Holy One of Israel stripping his people bare as he removes food, water, and leadership (vv. 1-5). There will be panic amongst the people (vv. 6-8), and all of their beauty will disappear (3:16-4:1). The Holy One of Israel has come to judge (3:13-14), and his people will know because of their dire circumstances. All of this is simply rebellion inviting its just reward, judgement.

This is sobering enough, but Isaiah's warning of judgement is not yet finished. Throughout Isaiah chapters 9 and 10 there is the fourfold repetition of these chilling words:

"For all this his anger has not turned away and his hand is stretched out still" (9:12, 17, 21; 10:4). This image conjures up the memory of being disciplined as a child. If the hand was raised again, you knew it was coming down again. For those first receiving Isaiah's message, this fourfold refrain would have served as a "recurring thunderclap that heralds the fierce storm of judgement."[3]

Perhaps one of the reasons that we avoid some vistas in Isaiah (and the Old Testament more generally) is because they paint a picture of God that is difficult for our modern sensibilities to accept. The God of judgement presented in these opening chapters of Isaiah is not one we like to talk about in contemporary society. Is it possible that a God of judgement is not one we want to believe in either? Isaiah's portrait of the Holy One of Israel, especially in these early chapters, poses the question: "Is your God too tame?"

Contemporary Christianity's portrayal of God is sometimes pathetic. It is like a grizzly bear, chained to a tree, dancing to some oriental music. In the wild this grizzly bear is powerful, majestic, and terrifying. In captivity it is pathetic. As Christians we all too often present a pathetic god. Isaiah's God, the God of the Bible is powerful, majestic, and terrifying. He is, after all, the Holy One of Israel. This ferocious judgement, then, is a timely reminder of the God-ness of God.

The theme of judgement, although unpalatable to modern ears, offers a vista not visited enough. It reminds us that disobedience and rebellion will not continue unabated. It asserts that there is a day, towards which we are moving

---

[3] Geoffrey W. Grogan, 'Isaiah', in *The Expositor's Bible Commentary*, Revised, 6 (Grand Rapids: Zondervan, 2008), 530.

steadily and in which all wrongs will be righted, wickedness eradicated, and righteousness celebrated. Our God will do this. But, before we begin sneering at those outside the church doors, remember these chapters are addressed to God's very own people. Israel is in the Holy One of Israel's cross hairs. This judgement of rebellion will be meted out on those who should be God's holy people. God's people are those who face the corrective outstretched hand because of their (our) rebellion against the Holy One of Israel.

I wonder, is your God too tame? If he never disagrees with you, if he never calls your actions into question, if he never redirects your path, then he probably is too tame. The vista of God's judgement exposes some scenes that are difficult to look at, but if God is to remain God, it must be one to which we return regularly.

Hope

Happily, the first twelve chapters do not end with judgement. Despite these opening twelve chapters being crammed full of the bad news of rebellion and judgement, at regular intervals they are punctuated by hope.

This hope is apparent almost immediately. The desperate judgement communicated in chapters 2 and 3 is bracketed by expressions of hope. Before the judgement is detailed, Isaiah communicates the hope of a renewed Zion (2:1-5), from which the word of the LORD goes forth (v. 3) and to which the nations will flock (v. 2). After the judgement is detailed, Isaiah communicates a day in which a "branch of the LORD" will appear (4:2-6). At the appearance of the phrase "In that day…" Isaiah's listeners and readers would have feared the worst (see 2:12-19). Surprisingly, however, instead of judgement it announces hope. This hope is an individual called the "branch of the LORD". The title always points to a royal-messianic figure promised by the Holy One of Israel.[4]   Remember, a significant element of the judgement was an absence of godly leadership. Thus, news of a promised royal-messianic figure means hope.

Towards the end of the first twelve chapters, this hope becomes more concentrated. It begins with the promise of a child, whose name will be Immanuel (7:14). There is some debate concerning the identity of this child in the context of Isaiah. As the prophecy continues to unfold, the child's identity becomes more intriguing and yet clearer at the same time. The child is soon "born" (9:1-7). In 9:6 the waters are muddied as the baby is ascribed deity by way of four titles: Wonderful Counsellor, Mighty God, Everlasting Father, and Prince of Peace. In 9:7, however, the child's identity is clarified; he will be a descendant of David and thus rightly an heir to the throne. He will be royalty. His identity is both intriguing and yet clear.

Clarity and intrigue appear again in chapter 11. This chapter reasserts all that has been mentioned previously. Hope is a child (v. 1); more, a royal child (vv. 1-5). He will usher in an idyllic rule and reign (vv. 6-9). Indeed, although he is a child, he is something more. Not only is this child the shoot (or descendant) of Jesse (v. 1) he is also the root (or source) of Jesse (v. 11). The turnaround in fortunes, from judgement to hope, is encapsulated by the outstretched hand of the Holy One of Israel (v. 11). Only the outstretched hand

---

[4] For a defence of this assertion see, J. Alec Motyer, *The Prophecy of Isaiah: An Introduction and Commentary* (Downers Grove: Inter-Varsity Press Academic, 1993), 65.

will save this time, rather than judge. This is hope.

The punctuated hope of these opening twelve chapters serves in a similar way to post-credit clips at the end of films. Marvel Studios persistently make use of the post-credit clip at the end of their films. Rarely does the clip advance the storyline of the film, however. Rather, it simply affirms the hope that there is another film to come. It confirms this is not the end. The hope that punctuates Isaiah 1-12 serves a similar purpose – the rebellion and judgement detailed here are not the end of the story. There is more to come. There is hope.

This hope is depicted in a variety of ways in these opening chapters. A renewed Zion (2:1-5), the word of the LORD (2:3), cleansing or washing (1:18), and a royal-messianic child (7:14; 9:1-7; 11:1-11). It is not until the New Testament that we observe this hope in the flesh. Matthew makes it unmistakeable in his Gospel as he quotes Isaiah 7:14 in relation to Mary's bearing Jesus (Matt. 1:23). Hope, promises Isaiah, is located in a child yet to be born. That child is Jesus. As the rest of Scripture testifies, it is only in and through Jesus that rebellion can be dealt with and judgement avoided. That is hope!

You will say in that day:
"I will give thanks to you, O LORD,
for though you were angry with me,
your anger turned away,
that you might comfort me.
"Behold, God is my salvation;
I will trust, and will not be afraid;
for the LORD God is my strength and my song,
and he has become my salvation."

12

With joy you will draw water from the wells of salvation.
And you will say in that day:
"Give thanks to the LORD,
call upon his name,
make known his deeds among the peoples,
proclaim that his name is exalted.
"Sing praises to the LORD, for he has done gloriously;
let this be made known in all the earth.
Shout, and sing for joy, O inhabitant of Zion,
for great in your midst is the Holy One of Israel."
(Isaiah 12:1-6)

THE HOLY ONE OF ISRAEL & THE NATIONS (ISAIAH 13-27)

Moral Minorities

I remain unconvinced that any country can be truly called a Christian country. Christianity may be the predominant religion, but that does not make a country Christian. That being said, it is fair to say that in previous eras the Christian worldview was once dominant in particular countries. This could be said of the United Kingdom. Here, Christian morals were once the measure of socially acceptable behaviour. This is no longer the case in the United Kingdom, and even in "backward" Northern Ireland. Bible-believing, evangelical Christians are no longer the moral majority. We are quite firmly the moral minority. In this, we might fear that we are facing circumstances that God's people never had to face before. This is not the case.

Israel may have been God's chosen people, but they did not live in isolation. Much like Christians today, Israel operated as the moral minority in the Ancient Near East.

14

Much like us, their lives consistently intersected with the world around them. Much like us, they had to learn to live a life of faith while rubbing shoulders with others who lived very different lives. The Holy One of Israel's people throughout the centuries have frequently found themselves operating as moral minorities.

Isaiah helps us in this, just as he helped Israel. Isaiah's focus moves from the Holy One of Israel and his relationship with his people (1-12), to his relationship with the nations (13-27). David Jackman reminds us: "The 'big picture' relevance to Isaiah's teaching is that all nations are equally under the sovereign control of the 'Holy One of Israel'."[1] We may be the moral minority, just like Israel, but we are not alone. We stand with the Holy One of Israel who controls all people, both those who are his and those who are not.

Humbled

Isaiah begins this second section of his prophecy with an oracle against Babylon (13:1-22). Babylon was to become one of Israel's fiercest enemies. They would eventually invade and ransack Jerusalem, carrying many of the people into exile and leaving the Promised Land languishing. It is not difficult to imagine how a strong nation like Babylon thought themselves impervious to attack as they systematically invaded and conquered other nations. They were the icing on the cake in the international political scene of their day. They were the top dogs.

But before any of this comes to pass Isaiah promises

---

[1] David Jackman, *Teaching Isaiah: Unlocking Isaiah for the Bible Teacher* (Ross-shire: Christian Focus Publications, 2010), 88.

Israel that this nation known as Babylon will one day be humbled. The Holy One of Israel's assurance to his people is this: "I will punish the world for its evil, and the wicked for their iniquity; I will put an end to the pomp of the arrogant, and lay low the pompous pride of the ruthless." (13:11). Indeed, the tool by which this will be accomplished is another nation, the Medes (Persians). The Holy One of Israel is stirring up the Medes (Persians; v. 17) to rip away the glory of Babylon (v. 19). Babylon will be so humiliated that they will be like Sodom and Gomorrah, never again inhabited (vv. 19-20).

The humbling of the Babylonians is no random affair of international politics. Isaiah has lifted the curtain to allow his listeners and readers to see that the Holy One of Israel is the one who directs the affairs of the nations. This point is reinforced with a taunt that Isaiah teaches the Israelites to sing in exile (14:4-21). Taunts were a powerful way to display defiance and hope while under the tutelage of an enemy nation (see Hab. 2:6-20). The taunt emphasises the same thing that Isaiah's oracle emphasised. The proud and arrogant, who believe they can ascend to the heavens and be enthroned with God (14:12-15), will be humbled. They will be so humiliated that they won't even enjoy the dignity of burial (vv. 16-20). Not only will Babylon be humbled, Moab will suffer a similar fate (15:1-16:14). Moab was also full of pride (16:6-7) and exhibited arrogance (12-14). But it will not be prolonged, for the Holy One of Israel will also humble them.

The reason that the nations will be humbled is pride. Once more Isaiah confronts us with a reality that is slightly unpalatable to our modern sensibilities. While we do not enjoy being in the company of proud people, we often believe that we are well within our rights to be proud ourselves. But we have developed a more sophisticated way of being proud – the humble brag. The humble brag is an attempt to appear self-deprecating, while also bragging about something of which we are proud. For example, "I just stepped on gum. Who spits gum out on a red carpet?" Do you see it? The individual walked on chewing gum (self-deprecating), but did so on a red carpet (bragging). Or, "I'm truly humbled you follow my tweets. I pray they enrich your life & strengthen your ministry. God bless all 200,000 of you!" You can't miss that one, can you? Why would anyone follow my twitter feed (self-deprecating), I love all 200,000 of you (bragging).

We might have a wry smile on our faces after reading that last paragraph, but pride is no laughing matter. As James makes clear, "God opposes the proud" (Jas. 4:6). Pride was the hallmark of Babylon, Moab, and numerous other nations on the international scene in Isaiah's day and the years that followed. It remains the hallmark of those looking in on the Christian moral minority today. They sneer at us, bragging about their enlightened views compared to the moral minority Christians stuck in the dark ages.

But God opposes the proud. Why? Because pride is satanic, it is a raising of oneself above one's station. Therefore, as we, the moral minority, face the onslaught of a proud and arrogant world we must realise that this is an expression of the power and influence that Satan is wielding in the world. Yet, we are not helpless as the Holy One of Israel is already humbling the proud and arrogant. Geoffrey Grogan insightfully observes: "It is a strange paradox that

17

nothing makes a being less like God than the effort to be his equal, for he who was God stepped down from the throne of his glory to display to the wondering eyes of men the humility of God."[2]   Humanity is created in God's image (Gen. 1:26-27), but as humanity attempts (in pride) to make themselves like God they become less like God as they become less human. This inversion occurs because God is a God of humility, expressed ultimately in his taking on flesh in the person of Jesus Christ (Phil. 2:5-8).

As the moral minority we must not be overwhelmed by the proud and arrogant society's shouting and finger-pointing aimed at us. Rather, we should pity them as they deface the image of God in their humanity and as we remember the Holy One of Israel will humble the nations. However, we must also be wary that we, as the moral minority, are not equally guilty.   Paul commanded the Colossian Christians to clothe themselves with humility (Col. 3:12) and the Philippian Christians to have Jesus Christ's same mind of humility (Phil. 2:5). We must be the humble moral minority.

Defeated

The Holy One of Israel will not simply humble the nations, but defeat them. This is the primary concern in this second movement of Isaiah, being repeated almost *ad nauseam*. It is well worth taking the time to read Isaiah 13-27 in one sitting to experience the repeated hammer blow of defeat on nation after nation.

After the humbling of Babylon and Moab, Assyria

---

[2] Geoffrey W. Grogan, 'Isaiah', in *The Expositor's Bible Commentary*, Revised, 6 (Grand Rapids: Zondervan, 2008), 565.

experiences defeat. The Holy One of Israel is uncompromising, he will break Assyria and trample it under his foot (14:24-25). Philistia is next, and rather than employing a metaphor, the Holy One of Israel simply states that he will kill Philistia (14:30). Damascus will be ruined by God, and in being ruined will cease (17:1). Cush will be exposed by God, left lying open to be plundered (18:4-6). Babylon's humiliation and defeat will be proclaimed as the news will spread, "Fallen, fallen is Babylon" (21:9). Even Jerusalem will face defeat for their rebellion detailed earlier in Isaiah (22:5-8). Tyre and Sidon will be laid waste (23:1).

It is truly a sobering portion of Isaiah's prophecy. Again and again and again; nation after nation after nation; defeat upon defeat upon defeat. The climax is reached in chapter 24 (pause and read it slowly) as Isaiah drives home that there is no escape from this defeat. Ultimate defeat is inescapable for the enemies of the Holy One of Israel. Like a nightmare in which you cannot outrun your assailant, so Isaiah makes it abundantly clear that no-one can outrun God's defeat of his enemies.

Isaiah proclaims a universal judgement that affects all. The Holy One of Israel's justice is comprehensive, there is no escape, no shade, no hiding place, no outrunning it. Pause to consider this. It does not matter who you are, where you live, or what you have done, if you remain an enemy of God there is no evading this defeat.

As the moral minority this should provoke two responses in us. First, it should provoke comfort. The moral minority will often be wronged, mistreated, misrepresented, and perhaps even persecuted to a greater or lesser degree. But those who remain unrepentant in their ungodly behaviour toward the moral minority will not escape. The Holy One of Israel will defeat them, and that should comfort us. Second, it should provoke compassion. Each member of the moral minority will know people who are enemies of God, will have family members who persist in rejecting God. Essentially, they are sticking it to God and fail to see the futility of their actions. We must have compassion for them in their ignorance, praying for them and pleading with them to see the Holy One of Israel for who he really is.

Resurrected

The compassion of the moral minority is not in vain. There is always hope. In a manner of speaking there is, for the nations, the hope of resurrection. There are subtle hints earlier in this movement of Isaiah that humiliation and defeat are not the only options for the nations. Most explicitly, even though Judah will suffer treachery at the hands of Babylon, there is the hope of restoration (14:1-2). A similar hope of restoration is offered to the nations of Cush and Egypt (18:7; 19:16-25). It seems that Cush and Egypt are representative of the nations as a whole.

It is towards the end of this second movement, however, that there emerges a sustained emphasis on the possibility of "resurrection" (25-27). The imagery that Isaiah uses is provocative. Calling to mind the renewed Zion (2:1-5), Isaiah describes a mountain on which the nations will gather to feast on a banquet provided by the LORD (25:6). Food is not all that will be enjoyed, for Isaiah proceeds to assure his readers that God will swallow up death, wipe away tears, and provide salvation (25:8-9). Not only is the imagery of nations feasting on the mountain of the LORD and death disappearing provocative, but so too is the scope of the recipients. There is a noticeable progression from all peoples in verses 6-7 (probably ethnic groups), to all nations in verse 7 (probably political groups that are likely smaller than ethnic groups), and finally all faces in verse 8 (individuals). The new life being promised here is just as comprehensive as the threat of ultimate defeat.

That is not to say that the humbling and defeating of the nations was an unnecessary show of strength by the Holy One of Israel. They are in fact the very means by which resurrection will be achieved. It is only by humbling the proud (26:5-6) that it can be said the dead will live and those in the dust will awake (26:19). The humbling of the proud and the defeat of the nations paves the way for resurrection. While the nations are primarily the recipients of this resurrection, God's people have an important role to play in it (27:6, 12-13). Pride and arrogance have been humbled and destroyed in death. The Holy One of Israel has swallowed death up, calling the dead to live. It is possible, then, for Israel now to fill the whole earth with fruit (27:6). This is quite a comeback. Having read Isaiah 13-24 we would be more than justified in thinking that the Holy One of Israel had turned his back on the nations. Yet, hope springs eternal in Isaiah 25-27.

Macauley Culkin made a similar comeback with an advert in December 2018. He shot to fame in the 1990s after starring in the first two Home Alone films. As often happens with child stars, too much money and not enough guidance led to a difficult life. I remember, throughout my teenage years, seeing pictures of this awful looking young man who used to be that cheeky Macauley Culkin. To all intents and purposes, it seemed like the end of the road for him. But, at

Christmas time in 2018 he made a comeback with an advert for Google in which he relived some of the Home Alone scenes with the help of a voice activated Google device. In a manner of speaking he had been "resurrected".

Among scholars there is debate about whether or not the Old Testament testifies to life beyond the grave. After all, this "resurrection" that Isaiah speaks of could just be a metaphor. It must be conceded that the Old Testament offers nowhere near the same amount of evidence as the New Testament for life after death. That being said, these chapters in Isaiah offer an often-neglected vista that points in the direction of life beyond the grave.

Isaiah makes it clear that death will be dealt with, it will be swallowed up by God (25:8). More, he specifically mentions that the dead will rise, those in the dust will awake (26:19). Bodies will be raised. The earth will give birth to the dead. The grave is not the end.[3] All of these statements take on added impetus because they follow the total defeat depicted in Isaiah 24. Indeed, the inclusivity of Isaiah 25-27 is also striking, as each and every nation who have been named and shamed in this movement, have hope held out to them. It is possible for the nations, if they respond appropriately to being humbled and defeated, to enjoy being resurrected by the Holy One of Israel.

Whether we face reward or punishment in the life beyond the grave, one thing is certain. We will come eye to eye with the Holy One of Israel. At that moment we will be all too aware of our humility and defeat, knowing our resurrection is at his mercy:

---

[3] J. Alec Motyer, *The Prophecy of Isaiah: An Introduction and Commentary* (Downers Grove: Inter-Varsity Press Academic, 1993), 219.

In that day man will look to his Maker, and his eyes will look on the Holy One of Israel. He will not look to the altars, the work of his hands, and he will not look on what his own fingers have made, either the Asherim or the altars of incense. (Isaiah 17:7-8)

THE HOLY ONE OF ISRAEL & HIS SOVEREIGN GRACE (ISAIAH 28-39)

Stalemate

The 2018 World Chess Final was a record breaker. After twelve games of chess it was stalemate. It wasn't that the two finalists had levelled the final at six games each. They had actually tied all twelve games. Neither finalist had won a game, and neither finalist had lost a game. The battle was so finely poised that neither could gain the upper hand. In fact, afterwards, in a press conference, one of the finalists explained that he never felt like he was losing, but equally he never felt like he was winning. It was stalemate.

From time to time, we are guilty of thinking about the battle between good and evil in a similar way. Or to put it more explicitly, we often think that the battle between God and Satan is a dead-heat, it is stalemate. God is prevailing here, while Satan is prevailing there. Neither really gaining the upper hand. Wrongly, we think that the battle between God and Satan is stalemate (if we haven't already given it to

Satan!).

That is not Isaiah's view of things, and the vistas of this third movement make this clear. For Isaiah, the Holy One of Israel has no equal. Whenever he exerts his power, might, and strength nothing can stand in his way. No political power, no spiritual power, not even the sin of his very own people. This unequalled power comes to the fore in Isaiah 28-39. This is not simply raw power though. This power is driven by his gracious purposes for his people. It is his sovereign grace. Alec Motyer explains that it is the aim of these chapters to "demonstrate that the Lord does actually rule world history and that, therefore, his as yet unfulfilled promises and purposes are sure."[1]

This third movement (28-39) of Isaiah is intimately connected to the preceding two (1-27). The themes of judgement against Israel and the nations are reiterated in this section. Israel is reminded of the judgement facing her in chapters 28, 29, 30, and 32, while the nations are reminded of the judgement facing them in chapter 34. The distinctive aspect of this third movement is the power that God exerts in accomplishing good for his people. Isaiah's emphasis here is the Holy One of Israel's sovereign grace.

Sovereignty

The sovereignty of the Holy One of Israel is set on display from the outset (29:13-24). Even though there are elements of judgement and grace, Isaiah makes it clear that it is the Holy One of Israel who is acting, and thus in control. He does this by way of the image of the potter (v. 16). Both

---

[1] J. Alec Motyer, *The Prophecy of Isaiah: An Introduction and Commentary* (Downers Grove: Inter-Varsity Press Academic, 1993), 227.

Jeremiah and the Apostle Paul make use of this image too (Jer. 18:1-11; Rom. 9:20-24). This image points to God's sovereignty. It is made explicit in Isaiah 29:23, however, as God declares that all of the good communicated in this portion of the prophecy is the work of his hands. The Holy One of Israel need ask no permission for what he will do. He simply acts, and all humanity can do is stand in awe (v. 23).

The point is reinforced in the following chapter (30:27-33). Here the great Assyrian king meets a Greater King, the Holy One of Israel. The description of this Greater King proclaims his sovereignty. He burns with anger; fire and fury come from his mouth (v. 27). He brings a judgement that none can escape (v. 28). Then, action. The Greater King speaks and moves (v. 30). The result is terror-stricken Assyrians, their great king is of no help to them now (vv.31-32). The political power has been brushed aside by the word and arm of the Holy One of Israel. No might can rival his.

The influence of the sovereign power of the Holy One of Israel continues into chapter 31. In this chapter Isaiah communicates how intimately involved his God is with current events. The Holy One of Israel will arise (v.2), dispose of nations with his hand (v. 3), and, like a lion or a hungry bird standing over its prey, he is immoveable (vv. 4-5). His plans and purposes will prevail. This is the sovereignty of the Holy One of Israel. He directs all that takes place. Of this chapter, Motyer writes:

> The Lord never merely reacts to events as if sprung on him. He has prepared all beforehand and is totally master of the situation. The merest movement of his hand (31:3) is sufficient to dispose of Judah

and its supposed helper, Egypt.[2]

There is no confusion: when the Holy One of Israel lifts himself up, the nations flee (33:3).

The Holy One of Israel is sovereign. This is the emphasis that Isaiah is weaving through his prophecy at this point. The Holy One of Israel possesses full authority and ability to do as he pleases. He is the potter, everything else is his clay to mould in whatever way he sees fit. He is the Greater King, against whom all other kings pale into insignificance and are ultimately impotent. He is orchestrating all things, and the slightest movement of his hand redirects all the individual parts according to his will. Absolutely sovereign is how Isaiah views God.

I remember when my wife, Tracy, and I took our friend to see the Ulster Orchestra. It is not really our cup of tea, but Nathan is into classical music and so we thought we would treat him for his birthday. For those who are interested, it was Ravel's piano concerto in G major. Some things really surprised me. I expected pageantry, but only from the orchestra. The vigorous applause from the refined audience startled me (especially because it contained some whoops and whistles). The ladies sitting beside and behind us, who had to be the first on their feet for every standing ovation, even when there wasn't one, were both amusing and intimidating. The pianist was incredible, and made the piano make some remarkable sounds. The thing that really surprised me, however, was the conductor. I imagined that conductors conducted orchestras with their hands, but this one conducted the orchestra with his entire body. Every

---

[2] Ibid., 253.

single part of him was moving, gesticulating, and instructing the musicians in front of him. It was mesmerising to watch, and by the end of the concert he was understandably dripping with sweat.

By way of contrast, this conductor aids our understanding of God's sovereignty. The Holy One of Israel is not conducting a mere 100 musicians. He is conducting everything; from the orbit of the earth to the direction of countries, rulers, events, and people, right down to the movement of molecules and atoms. It is all under his control, and he keeps it all in perfect harmony.

Isaiah is not spouting all of this for the sake of it. He is making God's sovereignty clear in order to encourage Israel. He wants Israel to trust the Holy One of Israel, even (or should I say especially) when things look out of control. Isaiah is seeking to offer his listeners and readers certainty, and that certainty is the Holy One of Israel's sovereignty. No matter what it looks like on the world stage, the political scene, or in our personal lives, nothing is out of control. The Holy One of Israel is conducting all things to his tune. At times I thought the Ulster Orchestra were out of tune, the blend didn't seem to be working. But one flick of the conductor's wrist began the crescendo, and once the orchestra reached the climax it all made sense. So too with the Holy One of Israel and his sovereignty. One day everything will make sense.

Graciousness

As we have already noted, this focus on God's power is not just for the sake of it. Isaiah is anxious to ensure that God's people know God exerts his power for their good. This is made explicit in 30:15, as the Holy One of Israel invites

28

repentance and trust. Chapter 30 is full of graciousness and tenderness. This is particularly apparent in verses 18-26. This portion begins with the Holy One of Israel promising to be gracious, merciful, and compassionate (v. 18). His grace is his sovereign determination to bless the undeserving. His mercy and compassion are his overflow of passionate love for his people. This leads to a life of blessing in God's presence (v. 20). It brings about God's direction (v. 21), providence (v. 23-25), and eradication of wrong (v. 26). But notice the tenderness of the Holy One of Israel in verse 19. Despite the persistent rebellion of his people, at the faintest whimper from his people the Holy One of Israel answers.

This tenderness is conveyed by the image of doting parents responding to every little noise, every exhale of air, every toss and turn of their new born baby. Despite the long, loud, high pitched wailing, the messy nappies that required a change of clothes for both baby and parent, and the first signs of original sin, the loving parent still answers each whimper from their child. The Holy One of Israel is gracious. He is tender with his children. Each and every whimper is answered.

Yet the grace of God abounds. The threat of Isaiah 1-12 was, in part, an absence of faithful and just leadership. The hope in those early chapters was a branch of the LORD, a royal child (4:2-6; 11:1-11). In Isaiah 32 those early allusions to a future king are made explicit. Behold, Isaiah proclaims, a king will reign in righteousness (32:1). There is a coming king who will rule with justice (v. 1). He will open eyes and bring understanding (vv. 3-4), while at the same time removing unrighteousness (vv. 5-8). God's grace ensures the coming of a king who will implement a reign of peace and blessing, healing and joy.

This is not necessarily some distant hope. The people pray for God's grace to be known (33:2-4), and the answer comes, "Your eyes will behold the king in his beauty" (33:17). Again, Isaiah describes a reign of peace and prosperity for God's people under the leadership of this coming king (33:17-24).

The Holy One of Israel's grace reaches something of a climax in this third movement in Isaiah 35. It is scandalous that this chapter is one of the lesser viewed vistas of Isaiah. In this chapter all that had previously been lost in judgement is restored. Abundance will be restored to what has become desolate (vv. 1-2). Strength will be restored to those who have become weak (vv. 3-4). Healing will come to those who have had to endure suffering (vv. 5-7). The pathway of holiness that leads back to Zion will be unmistakeable, full of joy, and resounding with singing (vv. 8-10). All that is lost will be restored.

Isaiah is pointing his listeners and readers toward the great reversal that will take place. At this point in the biblical narrative God's people are experiencing what the Narnians experienced under the curse of the White Witch. It was always winter, but never Christmas. In Narnia this was evidenced by the blanket of snow and ice that covered the land. But, just as the Narnians hear a rumour that Aslan is on the move, so Isaiah assures his listeners and readers that the Holy One of Israel is on the move. The evidence of Aslan's activity is the first thaw. Spring is in the air, life is beginning to grow, and eventually summer will arrive.

The same thing is happening in this third movement of Isaiah. There is a coming king, and he brings with him the grace of God that will reverse the winter that that God's people have been experiencing. The Holy One of Israel desires his people's good; more, he desires our ultimate good. He desires to bless us, to lavish us with his love and grace, and to remove all of our sin, shame, and sorrow. Isaiah promises this in chapters 28-39, and begins to describe some of the ways in which this will happen. The Holy One of Israel will employ his sovereignty to ensure his people enjoy his graciousness.

Isaiah says more, however. He assures his listeners and readers that the Holy One of Israel will deliver this good to his people. There are no "ifs" or "buts". There are no hurdles to be jumped. There are no standards to be met. It is grace. Our God desires our good, and will deliver our good.

Ultimately this is achieved as the Holy One of Israel sends the king of Isaiah 32 to win this grace through the cross. Surely, having the whole of Scripture available to us, we need no greater evidence than the life, death, resurrection, and ascension of Jesus to convince us that the Holy One of Israel both desires, and will deliver, our good. But it is still only "spring-time". It is blatantly apparent that all is not as it should be. The king's reign of righteousness is not yet manifested in all of its fullness. Even so, summer is coming, and we can be certain of this because of the Holy One of Israel and his sovereign grace.

Historical Interlude

An added difficulty in reading and understanding Isaiah in its totality is the historical interlude of chapters 36-39. These chapters are conspicuous in Isaiah because they are primarily narrative in a prophetic book and parallel the history

31

recorded in 2 Kings 18:13-20:19. They are not, however, out of place. This historical interlude further illustrates all we have already observed in this section of Isaiah. It records the siege of Jerusalem by Sennacherib, but it testifies to the sovereign grace of the Holy One of Israel. He is in control of all things, even the dreaded Assyrians (we have been told this already in 30:27-33). Despite the dire circumstances and the bleak outlook the Holy One of Israel, in his grace, turns the events of Isaiah 36-39 for the good of his people.

The Holy One of Israel is not giving it his best shot in the battle with evil and Satan. There is no stalemate here. Rather, the Holy One of Israel is playing the long game. All things are under his control and direction. In his grace he is working them for our good and his glory. One day soon the Holy One of Israel in all his sovereign grace is going to declare, "Checkmate!" And so, we pray:

> O LORD, be gracious to us; we wait for you.
> Be our arm every morning,
> our salvation in the time of trouble. (Isaiah 33:2)

THE HOLY ONE OF ISRAEL & HIS SERVANT (ISAIAH 40-55)

Mystery Guest

Did you know that the BBC quiz show "A Question of Sport" first aired in 1968? It has been on BBC television for over 50 years, and yet I have only ever known Sue Barker as the presenter. Apologies if that makes you feel your age a little more acutely.

One of the most difficult rounds on the quiz show is entitled, "Mystery Guest". The teams are shown a short video of some famous sportsperson dressed up and engaging in a random activity. Someone might be dressed up as a cowboy, with a Stetson pulled low over their eyes and a neckerchief pulled up over their mouth and nose. Someone else might be engaging in a bit of gardening, their face being covered by a mixture of shrubbery, trellises, and flowers. Someone else has gone for a spot of clay pigeon shooting, sporting a flat cap, those strange orange glasses, and always blocking their face with the butt of the shotgun. The teams are desperately attempting to identify the mystery guest, but to be honest they haven't got a lot to go on. Having said that, when the answer is revealed it is always obvious!

Isaiah 40-55 has its own mystery guest. In these chapters Isaiah reveals exactly how the Holy One of Israel is going to achieve all of the hope, grace, and restoration that has been promised in the opening 39 chapters. By way of four so-called "Servant Songs" (or better, poems) Isaiah communicates the reality that the Holy One of Israel's promised salvation will be won by his Servant. This is Isaiah's mystery guest. Who exactly is this Servant? Well, it is difficult to tell. This Servant often has a hat pulled low over his eyes, his face is frequently hidden behind a variety of obstacles, and even the clearer descriptions are coloured in a somewhat unnatural way. Nevertheless, there is also something strikingly familiar about these descriptions.

Each of the so-called "Servant Songs" contributes a different aspect to Isaiah's portrayal of the Servant. By the end of this chapter I hope we will have a clearer idea of who exactly this Servant is.

Spirit-Filled

The focus in this section of Isaiah is squarely on the Servant. However, we must not be fooled into thinking that the Holy One of Israel has disappeared. In fact, that can hardly be the case as Isaiah reiterates the Holy One of Israel's kingly power and sovereign might in chapters 40-41. The description of God in these chapters is both heart-warmingly encouraging and frighteningly humbling. The Holy One of Israel states explicitly that in his power and might he will help Israel (41:8-10, 14). Therefore, it appears that the Servant is God's agent in accomplishing the hope, grace, and restoration that the Holy One of Israel has promised earlier in Isaiah. It would seem that anything the Servant does is initiated, empowered, and fulfilled with the power of the Holy One of Israel.

The careful reader of Isaiah will have noticed that in 41:8-9 Israel is called "my servant" twice. This has led to some confusion about the identity of the Servant. A number of commentators argue that the Servant must be Israel, as elsewhere in Isaiah Israel is called "servant". This reasoning, as will soon become clear, falters in light of the content of the so-called "Servant Songs", the first of which is contained in Isaiah 42:1-9.

Immediately preceding the first "Servant Song" Isaiah warns his listeners and readers about the foolishness of idols. "Behold," he declares, "they are all a delusion; their works are nothing; their metal images are empty wind." (41:29). This is immediately contrasted with the Servant. In 41:29 Isaiah proclaims: "Behold, idols." In 42:1 he proclaims: "Behold, the Holy One of Israel's Servant." Rather than being an empty wind, the Servant is Spirit-filled.

The Holy One of Israel has put his Spirit on this Servant (42:1). This, however, is not simply asserted, but also demonstrated. The Spirit-filled nature of the Servant will be evident in the justice that he will bring (vv. 1, 2, 4). This Servant will do what many of Israel's rulers failed to do, rule with justice. This is certain because the Holy One of Israel will empower him to do so (vv. 6-9). The promises made to God's people in chapters 1-39 will begin to come to fruition in this Spirit-filled Servant as he brings forth justice.

A video referee at a rugby match or cricket test is able to watch the action in slow-motion, from a variety of angles, again, and again, and again. By doing so, the video referee should be able to make the correct decision, a just decision. This is the idea that Isaiah is conveying in this first so-called "Servant Song": the Servant will see everything correctly, make right pronouncements and so deliver justice. Fittingly, this leads to a response of praise (42:10-13).

Prophet

We have to wait until Isaiah 49 for the second so-called "Servant Song". The message throughout the intervening chapters (43-48) is that the Holy One of Israel, alone, will bring salvation to Israel. God's people are to look nowhere else but to God for salvation. Yet, as we have already mentioned, the Servant will be the Holy One of Israel's agent in this.

Isaiah 49:1-7 is the second so-called "Servant Song". In it the Servant prophetically highlights that the coming salvation will be through him (v. 5), and extend to the nations (v. 6). The prophetic element is highlighted at the outset of the song with the call to "Listen" (v. 1). Using the very same Hebrew term the Holy One of Israel has persistently called his people to listen to him or to hear him (for example, 48:1, 12, 16). By employing this same term, the Servant is claiming to speak with the authority of the Holy One of Israel.

The image of swords and arrows in verse 2 further assumes prophetic capacity in the Servant. This illustration reinforces the accuracy and penetrating power of the Servant's words. He will not miss; he will land the blows he intends to land. The calling of the Servant from the womb (vv. 1, 5) also evidences the prophetic aspect of the Servant's task. The language of these verses is echoed in Jeremiah's call (1:4-10). This Servant will be a prophet.

The calling from birth and the suggestion that the Servant is a prophet sheds further light on the identity of the Servant. It seems to be clear now that he is an individual, not a nation. He is called from the womb and operates as a prophet. More, the Servant is to go to Israel (v. 5) with the aim of restoring them and bringing them back to a right relationship with the Holy One of Israel. Surely the suggestion that Israel can go to Israel to bring them back and restore them lacks a certain logic. The Servant is an individual, prophetic figure.

The aim here in this second so-called "Servant Song", as Alec Motyer summarises it, is "a release from bondage into the freedom of truth and a pilgrimage, not of the feet, but of the mind and heart into the newness the Servant has brought about."[1] This newness is salvation for Israel and the nations (vv. 5-6). This message of freedom, newness, and salvation will not be accepted, however. This leads to rejection of the Servant (v. 7), a rejection that will become more explicit in a later song.

Obedient

The third so-called "Servant Song" is contained is Isaiah 50. The theme of this song is the Servant's obedience. This obedience does not occur in a vacuum, but is in direct contrast to Israel's disobedience. In Isaiah 1-12 Israel's disobedience was stated extensively. There are reminders in this fourth movement of Isaiah that this disobedience is not yet obsolete (42:18-20; 48:18-19). On the other hand, the Servant is perfectly obedient.

---

[1] J. Alec Motyer, *The Prophecy of Isaiah: An Introduction and Commentary* (Downers Grove: Inter-Varsity Press Academic, 1993), 383–84.

Although Israel is not named in this third so-called "Servant Song", the nation is certainly in view (50:1-3, 11). As the song opens the Holy One of Israel acknowledges the judgement that Israel is facing. Nevertheless, the rhetorical questions of these opening verses (vv. 1-3) make it abundantly clear that the Holy One of Israel is capable of reversing judgement. By way of contrast to disobedient Israel the perfectly obedient Servant enters the stage in verse 4. His perfection is exhibited as his mouth is instructed by the Holy One of Israel (v. 4), his ears hear the Holy One of Israel's teaching perfectly (v. 4),[2] and the distinct lack of rebellion on the part of the Servant (v. 5).

Perhaps unsurprisingly this perfect obedience will lead to further rejection (v. 5). Notice the escalation from the second song in which the Servant is deeply despised (49:7), to the third song in which the Servant is physically assaulted (50:6). Yet, he will be able to endure it as the Holy One of Israel once more helps his Servant (v. 7). With the Holy One of Israel's help the Servant will be all that Israel was not. He will do all that Israel could not. He will perfectly obey the Holy One of Israel.

Sometimes the strangest memories stick in my mind. One of those strange memories is my utter dislike of re-lacing shoes whenever I was in primary school. If, after getting a new pair of trainers, I got home to find that each shoe was laced differently I was exasperated. If, before going out into the back garden to kill my dad's plants with a football, a lace snapped when I was tying it, I was infuriated. I had an utter dislike for re-lacing shoes. Soon I realised that my younger brother loved it and was quite good at it. Gary could do what

---

[2] Contrast this with Israel's deafness in 42:18-19.

I didn't want to do, and in some ways what I couldn't do through lack of desire and patience. Isaiah is telling his listeners and readers that this is exactly what the Servant will do for Israel. He will be perfectly obedient when they cannot and will not.

Substitute

In the wake of the third so-called "Servant Song" there is understandably an atmosphere of anticipation. If the Holy One of Israel is about to empower his Servant to do all that Israel cannot do for themselves, then hope is alive. Excitement pulsates through chapters 51 and 52. God comforts his people, bringing hope, joy, gladness, and thanksgiving (51:3). This salvation will last forever (51:6, 8, 11). Zion will be a beautiful and strong city once again (52:1-10).

The manner in which all of this is achieved is relayed in the fourth so-called "Servant Song" (52:13-53:12). Here, it is made clear that this salvation will be brought about by the substitutionary suffering and death of the Servant. For many Christians this is a very familiar piece of Scripture, but the sophistication of the poetry is often overlooked.

This final "Servant Song" is divided into five stanzas, each consisting of three verses in our English translations. The pinnacle of the song is the middle stanza (53:4-6). This apex makes it explicitly clear that the Servant will be a substitute; each and every blow delivered against the Servant is because of us. The suffering of the Servant is emphasised in the stanzas before (53:1-3) and after (53:7-9) the pinnacle. The loneliness of the Servant in enduring this suffering is striking in these two stanzas. There is hope, however, as the song's introduction (52:13-15) and conclusion (53:10-12) both allude to the vindication of the Servant. Kings shall shut their mouths because this suffering Servant will be given an inheritance among the strong. There is a pyramid effect to the poem:

C Substitution (53:4-6)

B Suffering (53:1-3)   B` Suffering (53:7-9)

A Vindication (52:13-15)   A` Vindication (53:10-12)

The sophistication of the song is matched by the power of its imagery. With this powerful imagery Isaiah is proclaiming that Israel's salvation will come through the substitutionary suffering of the Servant. It will take the life of another to bring salvation.

From time to time I challenge myself to read a sizeable novel. One that I have tackled recently is *The Count of Monte Cristo*. In order to set up the plot of the book the central character, Edmond Dantes, is falsely imprisoned, placed in solitary confinement, and really has no hope of ever escaping. This reality is almost too much for him. Until one day, by chance, he makes contact with a fellow prisoner. He too is in solitary confinement, but by means of a secret tunnel they frequent each other's cells. This makes life in prison bearable. But tragedy strikes as the prisoner dies and Dantes is left alone once more.

This death, however, provides a way out of prison. Dantes, rather cunningly, removes his fellow prisoner's body from the body bag, and places him in the bed in Dantes' own cell. Covering up the secret tunnel, Dantes then secures himself inside the body bag. The prison guards come to remove the body from the cell, and unwittingly free Dantes. Only by the death of his fellow prisoner was Dantes able to escape (false) imprisonment. Isaiah is making it clear that it is no different with Israel. Only through the substitutionary death of the Servant can salvation flow to Israel, and the ends of the earth (52:10).

Revealing the Mystery Guest

After covering all four so-called "Servant Songs" it is time to play our own game of mystery guest. Who is the Holy One of Israel's Servant? Who is this individual who is Spirit-filled, a prophet, perfectly obedient, and a substitute? It seems to me that the New Testament makes it clear that it is Jesus.

The first song is actually quoted by Matthew in his Gospel (12:18-21). The point being made by Matthew is that Jesus' ministry was fulfilling the first so-called "Servant Song". Jesus and his ministry were Spirit-filled. The second song foreshadows Jesus' prophetic ministry. The Gospel accounts all present Jesus as speaking God's word to his people (for example, Matt. 5-7). The specific imagery of the Servant's prophetic words being like a sword are explicitly applied to Jesus by John in Revelation (1:16; 19:15, 21). The third song has the broad theme of obedience. This is something that Jesus attains (and more, cf. Matt. 5:17). It also speaks specifically of torture (50:6). This torture is symbolic of all that Jesus would face. The fourth song is frequently quoted in the New Testament. It is the passage from which Philip explains the gospel to the Ethiopian Eunuch (Acts 8:26-40). The Apostle Peter alludes to it in his first letter (2:22-25) as he writes about Jesus' substitutionary sacrifice on the cross.

It seems to me that the New Testament is clear about who our mystery guest is in Isaiah 40-55. He is revealed as Jesus of Nazareth, the Christ. Jesus is ultimately

41

the one who brings salvation to Israel, and the ends of the earth.

The Servant's Significance

There has been little application in this chapter as we have explored the so-called "Servant Songs" in the fourth movement of Isaiah's prophecy. I want to close, then, by making three brief comments about the Servant Songs' significance for us today.

First, the Holy One of Israel knows what he is doing. These so-called "Servant Songs" were written down at least 700 years before Jesus Christ walked the dusty roads of Galilee. The Holy One of Israel was in no doubt about the plans and purposes he was weaving together. He tells his people, albeit in a slightly veiled manner, about the plans and purposes he is weaving together. Then he is true to his word. The Holy One of Israel orchestrates his promises, reveals his promises, and keeps his promises. As we read Scripture today we will come across promises that have not been kept, as of yet. The so-called "Servant Songs" encourage us to trust that God knows what he is doing, and will finally keep those promises.

Second, the Holy One of Israel's salvation is a gift. This is pressed home in all of the songs to a greater or lesser degree. The salvation that the Servant brings is a gift. It is free. There is nothing Israel can do to save themselves. All that Israel can do is hold out their hands and accept the gift of salvation. This is a reminder that we need constantly. All too often we let ourselves forget this reality. We con ourselves into thinking that we have earned or deserved salvation in some way. The so-called "Servant Songs" remind us that it is only because of the Spirit-filled prophet, who in obedience suffered as our substitute, that we can enjoy salvation.

Third, Jesus is all that Israel should have been. In reflecting on the so-called "Servant Songs" it is blatantly apparent that Israel should have been all these things. Israel should have embodied the Spirit-filled justice of the first song. Israel should have spoken the Holy One of Israel's truth to the nations that surrounded them like the prophetic Servant of song two. Israel should have been the obedient son of the third song. Israel should have selflessly served the world at their own cost like the Servant in song four. It took the Servant, Jesus Christ, to be the True Israel. This ties up all of the promises made to ethnic Israel throughout the Old Testament in Jesus Christ. Consequently, they are reapplied to the church in the New Testament as they await the ultimate city coming down from above (Heb. 11:10; 13:14).

It is not surprising to realise that Isaiah closes this section by inviting everyone who thirsts to come and quench that thirst for free (55:1). More, he urges his listeners and readers to seek God's grace while it may be found (55:6-7). For if we do, we will go out in joy and be led forth in peace (55:12-13).

THE HOLY ONE OF ISRAEL AND HIS KINGDOM (ISAIAH 56-66)

Royal Antiques

Monarchs once dictated to their kingdoms. In the United Kingdom we have perhaps become unaccustomed to this reality. Today the Royal Family are treated more like an antique. They are to be kept on show, but not used in the way they once were.

The power that Monarchs once exercised can be effectively illustrated by considering the Reformation in England. Unlike the Reformation in continental Europe, which was led by individual figures such as Martin Luther, Ulrich Zwingli, and John Calvin, the Reformation in England relied heavily on the Monarch and their religious persuasion at any given time.

King Henry VIII, seeking a divorce, declared England to be Protestant, and England was then considered Protestant. He was followed by his son, Edward VI. Edward, however, was too young to rule in his own right and so a regency council consolidated the move toward Protestantism. Edward was followed by Queen Mary Tudor. Being Catholic, and remembering with bitterness the scandalous treatment of her mother by Henry, she declared England to be Catholic. England was once more considered Catholic. Mary was succeeded by Queen Elizabeth I who declared England to be Protestant, and England was Protestant again.

This was the power that monarchs once exercised in England. Whichever religious inclination they possessed soon became the religious inclination of the nation, whether enforced or willingly accepted. Despite being royal antiques now, Monarchs once exercised great power over their kingdoms. It is this image that Isaiah seeks to conjure in his listeners and readers as he draws his massive prophecy to a close.

Isaiah ends by drawing attention to the Great Monarch and his kingdom. Throughout this prophecy Isaiah has communicated cycles of judgement and salvation, expressions of the Holy One of Israel's sovereignty and graciousness, and the saving work of the Servant. Now he explains where all of this is leading, to the Holy One of Israel's Kingdom.

Righteous

Strangely enough, Isaiah begins his description of the Holy One of Israel's righteous kingdom by detailing sin. Toward the end of chapter 56 Isaiah refers to the poor leadership that Israel once more suffers (56:9-12). The real issue is picked up in chapter 57. The people have engaged in immoral and idolatrous acts (57:4-6). This sin has led to the Holy One of Israel leaving the people to cry out in futility to their idols for

45

deliverance (57:11-13). Israel have been charged, put on trial, and found guilty. The Holy One of Israel is clearly against these rebellious sinners.

Isaiah's purpose in these opening chapters of the fifth movement is to expose sin (cf. 58:1). Not only does he charge the people with sin, he explains where this sin will lead them (59:1-15a). In chapter 59 Isaiah asserts that sin will bring separation between the people and God (v. 2). It will lead to an absence of justice and peace (v. 8). It will ultimately bring blindness and its disastrous effects (vv. 9-10). Sin will lead to a very unhappy place.

None of this is the Holy One of Israel's fault, however. He has been kind, compassionate, and gracious; he was waiting with open arms but the people have rejected him (65:1-7). Yet, not everyone has rejected him. There are some within Israel who remain faithful, and they will be blessed, honoured, and welcomed into this righteous kingdom. In 65:13-16 Isaiah compares and contrasts these two groups of people; by doing so he sets a dull grimness alongside a delightful gloriousness. The wicked who reject the Holy One of Israel will go hungry and thirsty, be shamed and wail in torment. On the other hand, the faithful will be fed and watered, rejoice and sing for joy.

It is precisely this division that makes the kingdom righteous. Evil, sin, immorality, and idolatry will be excluded from this kingdom and all of its benefits. Righteousness, justice, obedience, and right worship will be included in the kingdom, and enjoy all of its benefits. There is a division, a line drawn that excludes some and includes others. This dividing line is not like a fence marking a boundary. Those who are excluded will not be able to peer over the top or through a gap in the panels. The dividing line operates more like a cliff edge. Those who are excluded drop off over the edge, never to be seen again.

The demarcation of this kingdom is not physical, it is spiritual. The Holy One of Israel's kingdom is not demarcated by geography, it is demarcated by people. This righteous kingdom is exhibited in the Holy One of Israel's righteous people. It follows that if this kingdom is righteous, and demarcated by righteous people, only the righteous will be granted entry.

This unexpected vista of a sharp division should cause us to pause and consider. This reality forces the listeners and readers of Isaiah to examine ourselves. Are we exhibiting a life of righteousness? This is not to say that we must be perfect. Rather, is our life characterised by righteousness? Do we demonstrate a pattern of righteousness in the way we think, act, and speak?

These questions are vitally important because there is no living on the demarcating line of the kingdom. There is no enjoying the blessings from a distance. We are either in or out (65:13-16). We are either on top of the cliff participating in the kingdom, or drifting out to sea never to be heard of again. Isaiah is unequivocal; the Holy One of Israel's kingdom is righteous and that means sinners will be excluded. Yet, careful readers of Scripture will soon realise that everyone is a sinner.

Redemptive

Happily, Isaiah proceeds to elaborate that the Holy One of Israel makes it possible for sinners to be forgiven, redeemed, and included in the righteous kingdom. The Holy One of Israel's kingdom is also redemptive.

The extent of this redemption is global. This was hinted at near the beginning of Isaiah with the promise of the nations flowing to Zion (2:1-4). In the opening chapter of this fifth movement the same global redemption is spoken of (56:1-8). When the nations flow to Zion the Holy One of Israel will accept them. This acceptance is in light of the salvation and deliverance sent and revealed by the Holy One of Israel (v. 1), and so the nations are welcomed to Zion (vv. 6-8). Those who join themselves to the Holy One of Israel and love him, minister to him, obey him, and hold fast to his covenant will be redeemed and included in the kingdom – no matter where they come from. This passage "portrays the gathering of people in which all are one, all are equal, all are welcome in the house of prayer."[1]

This global redemption will be achieved by the Holy One of Israel's salvation (56:1). Remarkably, Isaiah reiterates that the Holy One of Israel will win this salvation himself (59:15b-21). The Holy One of Israel will clothe himself with salvation (v. 17), and a Redeemer will appear in Zion (v. 20). These actions will make it possible for sinners to gain acceptance into the kingdom. Not everyone will gain entrance though. The Holy One of Israel also clothes himself with vengeance and zeal (v. 17), and wrath will be executed on his enemies (v. 18). Salvation is for those who recognise their sin and "turn from their transgression" (v. 20). This global redemption is secured by the Holy One of Israel and his Redeemer (v. 20; the Servant?). It is then enjoyed by the repentant.

This is a spectacular message; the righteous kingdom

---

[1] J. Alec Motyer, *The Prophecy of Isaiah: An Introduction and Commentary* (Downers Grove: Inter-Varsity Press Academic, 1993), 463.

can be enjoyed by sinners through the redemption provided by the Holy One of Israel. It is a message that must be proclaimed. Therefore, the Holy One of Israel sends a messenger to proclaim both the good and the bad news (61:1-4). The Holy One of Israel's messenger announces both a year of the LORD's favour and a day of God's vengeance. This is an announcement of a redemptive kingdom. Sinners are shown the way to enter the righteous kingdom, a kingdom of peace, justice, righteousness, and joy (61:8-11).

There is a swelling delight as Isaiah's listeners and readers come to see the Holy One of Israel's kingdom as redemptive. Even though we are sinners, it is possible to enjoy salvation and be granted access to the kingdom. This fifth movement of Isaiah makes it clear that this entrance into the kingdom is granted only by the king. Imagine exhausting yourself searching for a ticket to see your favourite band live in concert. No matter where you look, how long you look, or even how much you are willing to pay, there is no ticket to be had. The ticket cannot be bought for love nor money. Then you hear that it is possible to be granted entrance by simply turning up empty handed. All you have to do is acknowledge you cannot gain entrance yourself. You turn up on the evening, admit your inability to gain entrance in your own right, and you are handed a ticket by a generous doorman.

The Holy One of Israel's entrance requirements for his kingdom are the same. Entrance cannot be gained in your own right; access cannot be bought for love nor money. We simply turn up, confessing our own inability, and revel in the redemption we can enjoy. It is the Holy One of Israel who clothes himself with salvation, promises a Redeemer, and announces the good news of the year of his favour. Entrance to the kingdom is a gift, and in being a gift it is redemptive.

For Isaiah and his initial audience, they had to look forward to this redemption. For us, we look back and marvel at the magnificent way in which the Holy One of Israel ensured redemption for all nations in his Redeemer. A redemption accomplished by who Jesus is, and all that he has done and continues to do. Entrance into this redemptive kingdom is a gift of grace. We do not deserve and we cannot earn entrance, but the Holy One of Israel handed us a ticket at the door when we stood empty-handed.

Flawless
Often free things are substandard, but not this kingdom. Although entrance is a free gift, it is not to be spurned because the Holy One of Israel's kingdom is flawless. It is something we want to be part of.

The Holy One of Israel's kingdom is one of glory and majesty. In chapter 60 Isaiah eloquently describes the radiance of this kingdom (vv. 1-5). No longer will conflict and violence be inflicted by enemies, for they will be vanquished (vv. 10-14). The glory of the Holy One of Israel will be the shining light of this kingdom (vv. 19-22). It is difficult to imagine a kingdom of this quality.

The kingdom is further described in Isaiah 62. There the memory of judgement in earlier chapters is stirred up again as Isaiah reminds Zion that it was once named "Forsaken" and "Desolate" (62:4). But there are new names given to Zion now, "Sought Out" and "A City Not Forsaken" (62:12). These new names reflect the reality of the Holy One of Israel's kingdom. There is a new dignity to this kingdom.

Zion's transformation merely points forward to the full manifestation of the Holy One of Israel's flawless kingdom. The magnitude of this kingdom is communicated in Isaiah 65:17-25. It is going to abound with blessing and silence sin. The whole of creation will be populated with the Holy One of Israel's glad subjects and so all of it will be his domain. This is nothing less than the new heavens and the new earth that Isaiah is describing:

> "For behold, I create new heavens
> and a new earth,
> and the former things shall not be remembered
> or come into mind.
> But be glad and rejoice forever
> in that which I create;
> for behold, I create Jerusalem to be a joy,
> and her people to be a gladness.
> I will rejoice in Jerusalem
> and be glad in my people;
> no more shall be heard in it the sound of weeping
> and the cry of distress.
> No more shall there be in it
> an infant who lives but a few days,
> or an old man who does not fill out his days,
> for the young man shall die a hundred years old,
> and the sinner a hundred years old shall be accursed.
> They shall build houses and inhabit them;
> they shall plant vineyards and eat their fruit.
> They shall not build and another inhabit;
> they shall not plant and another eat;
> for like the days of a tree shall the days of my people be,

and my chosen shall long enjoy the work of their hands.
They shall not labor in vain
or bear children for calamity,
for they shall be the offspring of the blessed of the Lord,
and their descendants with them.
Before they call I will answer;
while they are yet speaking I will hear.
The wolf and the lamb shall graze together;
the lion shall eat straw like the ox,
and dust shall be the serpent's food.
They shall not hurt or destroy
in all my holy mountain,"
says the LORD. (Isaiah 65:17-25)

This is *the vista* of Isaiah!

Thomas More is famous for writing the novel *Utopia*. The reader is introduced to an individual called Raphael Hythloday who recounts a visit to an island called Utopia. He proceeds to describe what More imagines might be an ideal society. One in which everyone lives in harmony, working for the good of each other, and enjoying perfect peace. The flawless kingdom that Isaiah describes could rightly be called Utopia. It will be radiant in glory, filled with the Holy One of Israel's presence, and exude perfection in innumerable ways. It will, in essence, be flawless.

By speaking of a new creation Isaiah makes it clear that it will take a cataclysmic event to bring this kingdom about. Consider the world we live in. It is not flawless. The Holy One of Israel will have to create once more. This re-creation is not an individual event, it is a cosmic event. Drew Hunter highlights that "While the focus of redemption throughout the Bible is often on God's graciousness to forgive and reconcile individual human beings, it is more broadly a plan for the whole cosmos."[2]   We need to grasp this larger vision.

The Apostle Paul alludes to this in Colossians as he writes about Jesus reconciling all things to himself through his death on the cross (1:20). This is not universalism, but rather a reconciliation of the whole created order by making it anew. It is the full manifestation of the Holy One of Israel's kingdom in the new creation.

For the Christian, this means that our ultimate hope is not tied up in this world. Our ultimate hope is not tied up in the things we experience with our five senses. Rather, our hope is tied up in something yet to come in all of its fullness. Our hope is tied up in new heavens and a new earth that are flawless. Our hope is tied up in new heavens and a new earth that are redemptive because only God's people will be there. Our hope is tied up in new heavens and a new earth that are righteous because all sin and evil will be vanquished. The Holy One of Israel's kingdom is where our hope is located, and that is the direction that Isaiah has been pointing us in for 66 chapters.

---

[2] Drew Hunter, *Isaiah*, Knowing the Bible (Wheaton: Crossway, 2013), 88.

CONCLUSION:
VISTAS OLD AND NEW

It is a good thing to have old vistas that are familiar. To be able to close your eyes and picture in your mind's eye those familiar vistas that bring comfort and awe is a gift. This short book is not a plea to forget the familiar vistas of Isaiah. Rather, it is a plea to add new vistas to existing ones. This, however, is not an easy task.

To the vista of Slieve Donard I can add Victoria Falls in Zimbabwe. During my time at Bible College I was required to complete a cross-cultural placement. In 2012 I had the privilege of completing this in Harare, Zimbabwe with Central Baptist Church. Although most of my time was spent in Harare, Tracy and I made it to Victoria Falls toward the end of our time there. To enjoy this new vista, we had to take three flights (Belfast-Dubai-Harare) covering nearly 10,000 miles to first find ourselves in Zimbabwe. Once there it took an additional a day-long coach trip covering a further 550 miles. There was also a short walk from our hostel to the falls. It was hard work to make it there, but it was worth it.

If you have been reading large chunks of Isaiah alongside this book you will be aware of the difficulty of the task of adding new vistas to existing ones. Isaiah is long, sometimes obscure, and largely unfamiliar. Nevertheless, there are vistas of glory, holiness, redemption, grace, and hope that must be discovered and remembered. It will be hard work, but it will be worth it.

Over five movements Isaiah explains that the Holy One of Israel's relationship with both his people and the nations needs repairing. Mercifully, these reparations will be initiated by the Holy One of Israel for he is both sovereign and gracious. The agent of the reparations is a mysterious figure known as the Servant, and he makes it possible for the Holy One of Israel to establish his kingdom. It is all about the Holy One of Israel and his actions for our good, and so we close by praying a prayer based on Isaiah 63:15-64:12 that seeks God's actions for our good:

Holy One of Israel, look down from heaven and see. Where is your zeal and your might? Where is your compassion? Abraham might not know us, and Israel may not acknowledge us, but you are our Father and Redeemer. We have wandered away, failing to fear you, and behaving like those who do not know you.

Oh, would you rend the heavens and come down. Act in your might so that the mountains quake. Make your name known among the nations, cause the world to tremble at your presence. Open ears, open eyes, ignite memories, and blot out sin. We are unclean, unrighteous, full of sin and iniquity. We have neglected to call on your name, and you have rightly hidden your face from us.

But now, we confess you are God. You are the Potter, and we are your clay. You are the Craftsman, and we are the work of your hands. We humble ourselves before your majesty and ask that you would not remain angry. Do not remember our sin forever. Look down from heaven and see our repentance.

Please do not restrain yourself from acting. Please do not remain silent. Please do not let our affliction continue. Holy One of Israel, we ask that you would look down from heaven and see us, break open the heavens and return. Bring forth new heavens and a new earth, and grant your people access to this flawless kingdom.

In the Servant's name, and for the glory and majesty of the Holy One of Israel, answer our prayer.

POSTSCRIPT:
THE BOOK OF ISAIAH

The Man

The book of Isaiah is almost silent in terms of Isaiah the man. Even the introduction, "Isaiah the son of Amoz" (1:1) is unenlightening. The only significant piece of personal information that is communicated to the reader of Isaiah is his call in chapter 6. Only here do we glimpse an insight to the man Isaiah as he records the powerful vision that led to his prophetic ministry. The New Testament witnesses to Isaiah's prophetic foresight (John 12:37-41) and to his boldness (Romans 10:20). Hebrews 11:37 possibly alludes to Isaiah's death, as Jewish tradition suggests that he was sawn in two by King Manasseh. Nevertheless, Scripture's sole interest is Isaiah's message, not his person.

The Times

Isaiah's times were a watershed moment for God's people. His ministry took place during reigns of four kings: Uzziah, Jotham, Ahaz, and Hezekiah (1:1). These kings all reigned in

Judah, and the totality of their reigns amounts to more than 100 years (approximately 790 B.C.E. – 680 B.C.E.).

It is possible to propose a tighter timeline for Isaiah's ministry. Isaiah's call to ministry took place in the year that king Uzziah died (6:1). It is widely agreed that 740 B.C.E. is the year that Uzziah died. This offers a start date for Isaiah's prophecies. Later, Isaiah records the death of Sennacherib (37:38). This is dated around 681 B.C.E. Although we cannot be certain that Isaiah's ministry ended at this point, it at least provides a 60-year window in which we can be certain Isaiah was active.

In this window the northern kingdom (10 tribes), known as Israel, falls to Assyria. This is alluded to and referenced in the early chapters of Isaiah. The southern kingdom, known as Judah, constituted the remaining tribes and maintained its independence for a little longer. However, their fall and exile are on the horizon. In later chapters, Isaiah warns Judah of this imminent danger and offers hope to sustain them in it. These details help us place Isaiah in a historical context.

The Theology

The Holiness of God – This point has been made by the title of this book and in the first chapter. One of Isaiah's concerns is to highlight the utter uniqueness of God's character. Namely, his holiness. He does this by way of the title "Holy One of Israel" (1:4; 5:19, 24; 10:20; 12:6; 17:7; 29:19; 30:11, 12, 15; 31:1; 37:23; 41:14, 16, 20; 43:3, 14; 45:11; 47:4; 48:17; 49:7; 54:5; 55:5; 60:9, 14). Additionally, he uses "Holy God" (5:16) and "Holy One" (10:17), as well as recording the seraphim's cry "holy, holy, holy" (6:3). Isaiah wants his listeners and readers to know God is holy.

The Sovereignty of God – This point is dealt with in chapter three of this book. Isaiah desires to impress upon his listeners and readers that God is sovereign. This is the reality for Israel, Judah, and the nations. God rules over all with might, power, and authority. The most potent display of this is Isaiah 40-41.

The Redemption of God – This point is elaborated in chapters three and four of this book. At a vital moment in Israelite history, on the verge of national disaster of the greatest degree, Isaiah assures the people of God that he is capable of redeeming them (43:1-28; 52:13-53:12). Indeed, God's people will be known as "redeemed ones" (35:9; 51:10; 62:12; 63:4). God is the one who is the redeemer (41:14; 43:14; 47:4; 48:17; 54:5).

The Spirit of God – No other Old Testament writer has more to say about the Spirit than Isaiah (11:1-2; 32:15; 34:16; 40:7, 13; 42:1; 44:3; 48:16; 61:1; 63:10, 11, 14).

ABOUT THE AUTHOR

S. David Ellison completed his Bachelor of Divinity in 2013 (Chester University/Irish Baptist College) and Master of Theology in 2016 (Queen's University, Belfast/Irish Baptist College). He is currently undertaking doctoral studies with Queen's University, Belfast and the Irish Baptist College in Old Testament Biblical studies. For good measure he also holds a Bachelor of Science in Geography (2009, Queen's University, Belfast).

In addition to his studies, David has served in the youth department of the Association of Baptist Churches in Ireland and in pastoral roles in a number of Irish Baptist Churches. In November 2019 he will take up the role of Training Director of the Irish Baptist College.

Currently David lives in Antrim, Northern Ireland with his wife Tracy. He is an elder in Antrim Baptist Church.